Angels Love Children

STORIES, POEMS, PRAYERS, & OTHER FAMILY FUN

by Herbert Brokering

Augsburg
MINNEAPOLIS

To you
angels of all ages and sizes
shapes and dimensions
colors and spheres
who keep alive
healing and love

ANGELS LOVE CHILDREN
Stories, Poems, Prayers, and Other Family Fun

Copyright © 1997 Augsburg Fortress. All rights reserved. Except for brief quotations in critical articles or reviews, no part of this book may be reproduced in any manner without prior written permission from the publisher. Write to: Permissions, Augsburg Fortress, 426 S. Fifth St., Box 1209, Minneapolis, MN 55440.

Scripture quotations unless otherwise noted are from the New Revised Standard Version Bible, copyright © 1989 by the Division of Christian Education of the National Council of the Churches of Christ in the U.S.A. and used by permission.

Scripture quotations noted Living Bible are taken from *The Living Bible*, copyright © 1971. Used by permission of Tyndale House Publishers, Inc., Wheaton, IL 60189. All rights reserved.

Art by Charley Rosengren adapted from Wheat Ridge Ministries Lutheran Wheat Ridge Christmas Seals '96.

Library of Congress Cataloging-in-Publication Data
Brokering, Herbert F.
    Angels love children : stories, poems, prayers, and other family
fun / by Herbert Brokering.
      p. cm.
    ISBN 0-8066-3333-6 (alk. paper)
    1. Angels—Prayer-books and devotions—English. 2. Devotional calendars.
3. Children—Religious life. I. Title.
BT966.2.B735 1997   97-44721
235'.3—dc21   CIP

The paper used in this publication meets the minimum requirements of American National Standard for Information Sciences—Permanence of Paper for Printed Library Materials, ANSI Z329.48-1984.   ∞

Manufactured in the U.S.A.   AF 9-3333

Contents

A Word from the Author

Several years ago, a friend called me, a teacher at a neighboring church school. "Herb, will you help our 200 children at St. Peter's to be more creative in their writing?"

"I will," I answered. And I did. We drew and wrote about angels for five days. I think the children enjoyed the experience as much as I did.

They drew what they did not see. Hundreds of angels. Then, while looking at their drawings, they wanted to talk and write and tell stories and ask questions. First they imaged, then they wrote and told and asked. So it is with the child's mind, so it is with us all. We image and then we talk and ask.

The 200 children are the inspiration for this book, *Angels Love Children*. They drew angels as belonging to real life.

In that week of drawing, I saw that children love angels of all kinds and for all kinds of reasons. Why do children love angels? I decided it is because angels love children.

Angels are the many messengers of God, visible, invisible, heavenly, earthly, young, old. They come in as many forms as there are light waves and sound waves and seasons and needs and wants. Angels have their own unique shapes and colors, as does everything else in God's creation.

When I was little, we were not skeptical about angels. We believed God had single angels, ones who came in pairs, and hosts of them. We did not argue about their style or looks or numbers. We looked for them and saw them. Even when we did not look, we saw angels. Angels gathered around our beds at night and we were safe as could be. And they were there in the morning, and they stayed with us through the day.

The 200 children inspired the reflections on the thirty angels in this book. I honor what they saw and said—and, more often, did not say. A halo was on the children as they drew.

Sometimes they drew and colored slowly. Some finished quickly. With a few words, I often sent the children back to add more to their drawings, to decorate, to write. *Draw in one more surprise. Play with shapes and colors. What are your angels doing? Draw in one more secret idea. Draw something so you can hear it, or feel the sound. Pretend what you are drawing is talking to you.*

Here are just a few examples of the hundreds of drawings and thousands of words we shared, as children showed me how much Angels Love Children.

Timmy drew someone sawing down a great green tree. An angel stands on the other side of the tree to stop the sawing.

Down the center of one page is a wall with steel barbed wire. Flags of enemy nations are on each side. Soldiers in helmets face each other. A wounded American lies on the ground. The angel with large, flowing wings speaks, "Now be good!"

Katy's angel was done in pencil. In a rectangle she printed, "War in angel wings." She drew stick-people inside an angel's two large wings. She wrote, "The war is going on and the angel is in the middle stopping it."

Sarah's angel is light yellow, trimmed in pink. She wrote, "Madness and mean ways shall be led to peace by the candlelight held by an angel!" The candlelight is all over her yellow angel.

One girl drew an angel on a teeter-totter with a soldier. She wrote the rules, "Whoever gets the other person up in the air, wins. No cheating." In the corner, a scoreboard reads, "Peace angel 6,000,000,000,000. War 0."

A boy drew awesome clusters of death—of persons and in nature. In the center, an angel is surrounded by dim images of flowers in green, pink, purple, blue. On the back of the drawing, the boy wrote: "This is after a war, and God's angel is bringing flowers, trees, and bushes back to life!"

Natalie's drawing is soft; I had to hunt for the candle markings and the yellow light over the page. She wrote: "The Light. God sent down the angels one by one, each holding a candle. A candle of love that would melt away the war of the world."

Chris's picture shows God in a tiny red cloud, and three angels stand smiling over a double rainbow. He wrote: "A kid is on his way up to hevin. He will like it in hevin. I will like it in hevin. You will like it in hevin! I love you God!!! I love you Jesus!!! The End."

Bethany's picture shows an angel with double wings, and a bouquet in a yellow vase on a blue table. God wears a crown and stands beside the angel. A gravestone below, at the edge of the sky, reads, "Grandma. 1995." Bethany wrote, "The angel is getting ready for a new girl in heaven. She is so happy."

Jackie drew an angel on skis being pulled carefully by its wings through a flower garden high on a green mountain.

Hannah's yellow angel nearly fills a huge red heart, broken in the center. All around are oval-shaped grave markers and rubble. Couples are dancing and sleeping safely in the corners of the heart. Her angel is a guardian.

Another child drew a party on a cloud. Angels ride across high waves in boats and canoes, and on water skis. Fish and pigs fly up to the party on the cloud. An angel riding a flying dolphin holds a cake of candles overhead.

Shannon drew an angel leading cats and dogs and lions with wings. A building in her picture has the name, "Pets and Co." The angel is calling "Here, Muttly," which is the name of her dog.

Kay Lee drew an angel high above a blue cloud, saying, "I'm jumping." Next to the angel a brown dog with yellow wings is barking, "I'm flying."

Alexandra's winged angel is pushing a doorbell at the entrance of heaven, which is a very large rainbow arch. A green sign reads, "Welcome To Heaven."

Jesse's angels are on skateboards zooming along a very high, looped track with "Heaven" marked on each end.

Jordan drew two angels pressing a broken world back together. He wrote, "Put the world together and glue it with love."

From the hundreds of drawings, I selected thirty to write about in a booklet of Advent devotions for Wheat Ridge Ministries. Artist Charley Rosengrin took the children's pictures and my thoughts one step further, creating illustrations for the booklet and for Wheat Ridge Christmas Seals. Those Advent devotions were remolded and expanded into the "Stories, Poems, Prayers, and Other Family Fun" in this book.

Ways to use the thirty devotions in this book.

The ideas inside are perfect for all shapes and sizes of families—including "families" of friends and families of one—and for all kinds of occasions. Each four-page angel "chapter" begins with words about the child's drawing and the reflections the drawing triggered in my mind. Then I hand things over to you. Use the *I wonder* and *What if* sections and the definitions ("A rainbow is . . . ") to spin off discussions, reactions, idea-sharing. One good question can open you to a new world of God's angels! Have fun with the suggestions for things to do. Take turns reading the prayers, or join hands and read them together.

When and why to use the book

- ♥ Use it whenever your family meets to talk and pray.
- ♥ Read parts during seasons of holy days.
- ♥ Use the book at bedtime story time.
- ♥ Read chapters at family gatherings and reunions.
- ♥ Use the book to explore the spiritual journeys of your children.
- ♥ Let the book help you keep alive your own family stories.
- ♥ Pull it out at a party for smiles and thought-teasers.
- ♥ Read parts alone when you're needing wonder and awe.
- ♥ Grandparents can use it to grow closer to their grandchildren.
- ♥ Read the book in a group talking about angels.

Angel of Rainbows

*Surrounded by rainbows
and colors of God,
An angel remembers
the words God has said;
The thoughts of God's promises
fill up its wings,
Its body, its feet,
its hands and its head.*

One little girl drew the shape of an empty angel: a head, two big wings, a flowing body, hands and feet. But it was just an outline. There was nothing inside. Then she leaned over her paper and quickly filled the angel with bright rainbows.

Not everyone can hear rainbows. I learned to hear rainbows—to listen to them—when I was little. While I stood on the porch with my father at the end of a storm, he'd say, "Listen. Listen." We'd look at the rainbow together, and I'd hear him say the words of God from the story of the flood: "Never again will a flood destroy the earth." Watching a rainbow was like hearing God say, "Herbert, I will not destroy you. I will save you."

That was the early meaning of rainbows for me. They were a picture of God saving us. The rainbow was my early picture of God in the clouds.

Nature is part of God's language of love. We read about God's love in the Bible, and then we find saving messages recorded in the world around us. A rainbow is God's word of love to the world. Season after season, nature sings as it repeats what God promises in the Bible. The rainbow is a Christmas picture, an Easter picture, a Valentine in the sky. God's love can be felt in the wind, it can be seen in the new, green shoot off an old stump, or in a twinkling star.

For ten years I took hundreds of people on tours of churches on the other side of the world's Iron Curtain, where it was often dangerous to be a Christian. In each journey we took beautiful rainbow cloth with us. We cut off tiny pieces of the cloth and gave them to the people we met in those churches. And we repeated God's promise: "I will not destroy you. I will love you and save you." The pieces of rainbow cloth are still with them—hanging on their walls, tied to their bedsteads, pressed in books as bookmarks. Reminders of God's love.

The little girl drew an angel and filled it with rainbows. Angels, messengers of God, absorb God's beautiful promises into themselves, so they believe from head to toe the promises of God they've come to know.

I wonder . . .

- 💟 how many colors make a rainbow.
- 💟 who has never seen a rainbow.
- 💟 how long a rainbow stretches.
- 💟 where a rainbow touches the earth.
- 💟 why rainbows need a cloud.

What if . . .

- 💟 a rainbow was part of our Christmas decorations?
- 💟 we had church service under a rainbow?
- 💟 people phoned their best friend when they saw a rainbow?
- 💟 rainbows could stay for a whole day?
- 💟 you could hear a rainbow whisper?

A rainbow is . . .

- 💟 a word of God stretched through the sky.
- 💟 a promise to my family.
- 💟 a cloud that has good news.
- 💟 a thought of God in technicolor.
- 💟 a picture too big for a book.
- 💟 a bridge under which to feel safe.

A rainbow poem to read and illustrate

"I have placed my rainbow in the clouds as a sign of my promise until the end of time, to you and to all the earth."
Genesis 9:12-13 (Living Bible)

If rainbows were circles and I were inside,
I'd have not a worry and nothing to hide.
If rainbows were arches all over my bed,
I'd sleep with a smile and with peace in my head.
If rainbows were pictures from God in the sky,
I'd see the next rainbow before it goes by.
If rainbows were bridges on which I could walk,
I'd go on these skyways and hear angels talk.
If rainbows were ribbons God tied to a cloud,
I'd thank God for nature and say it out loud.

Prayer

Today I will see something in nature as a sign of God's good news to me in the world, and I will say inside myself: To God be the glory.

O God, when a cloud is too dark, show me a rainbow in the cloud. When a thought is too sad, show me a rainbow in the thought. When I feel angry, show me a rainbow in my mind. When I feel down, show me your rainbow above me, and make me your own. Amen.

Angel of Hearts

*Angels go looking
for hearts in the sky.
Love is on earth
and Jesus is why.*

*Angels keep looking,
and hearts open wide
To peace and goodwill
and God's angel inside.*

A tiny, freckle-faced girl with bright red hair drew a universe, everything she ever knew that God created. I thought she was done when she put an angel in the very center of her universe. She stepped back to look at her picture. But then she frowned and bent over the paper again. She drew one long line around it all. A giant heart. And she outlined the heart in dark red. Then she put down her crayon, stepped back, and smiled. "That's God's heart," she told me. "And that's God's angel to watch over the whole world."

In Poland, where Christians like crosses, I bought a cross with a heart molded into its center. The heart is open, I can see inside; it looks alive. This is my only cross with a heart. It is my sign of the cross and the heart of Jesus.

When I was little we learned a prayer to sing: "Come into my heart, Lord Jesus." It was a comforting picture for me. In my heart is where I hid secrets. In this song and prayer I invited God to know me, to know the secrets in my heart.

I loved Valentine's Day when I was a child. I can still smell the paste, feel the scissors pressing on my thumb, as I carefully cut out fat and thin red hearts. How glad I was when the valentine heart looked perfect. All the while I cut I thought of the person for whom I was making the heart. The person was inside the heart I was making.

When I was a teenager, my heart had secrets and was filled with feelings. That same prayer, "Come into my heart, Lord Jesus," was still good for me. I could sing it with tears or laughter. The thought of God in my heart was awesome, for that is where I lived. That is where I dreamed, I imagined, I believed. I pictured God inside this room of mine, alone with me in my secret room.

At the same time I had another picture: I am in the heart of God. I thought, the heart of God must be a very large heart. God's heart was also the home of my family, friends, congregation.

I knew I was in the heart of my family and Mr. Haecker, Mrs. Hertlein, Irwin Cramer, Loretta Beck, and lots more people in my church. I knew they loved me, and I loved them. The picture of the heart kept my believing mind busy.

I still know the feeling I had when we cut out valentine hearts and pasted them on white doilies and wrote special words for someone we loved. The heart is a room for love.

A child drew a picture of love: a world and an angel—both inside God's heart. I do believe that God is in my heart, and that the whole world is in God's heart of love—along with God's angel of hearts.

I wonder . . .

- ♡ how God's heart looks.
- ♡ how God can be in us and we can be in God at the same time.
- ♡ why God loves us so much.
- ♡ if you can change your heart the way you change your mind.
- ♡ how our family looks inside God's heart.

What if . . .

- ♡ Valentine's Day was a holy day of the church?
- ♡ we sent a valentine to an enemy in another place or land?
- ♡ one day all soldiers in the world exchanged cookies shaped like hearts?
- ♡ people could say what's on their heart and still stay in love?
- ♡ I could know all the things God feels about me?
- ♡ we could see inside God's heart?

The heart is . . .

- ♡ where feelings can play hide and seek.
- ♡ where our thoughts get their energy.
- ♡ where worries can pile up and get swallowed up by God's love.
- ♡ the door to a medicine cabinet inside us.
- ♡ a room in which God visits us.
- ♡ where we keep our best pictures and poems.

Hearts for giving away

Cut out some bright red valentine hearts. On each, write a one-sentence love note. Then give the hearts away to secret pals and family friends, tuck them inside lunch bags and briefcases, hide them under dinner plates and pillows.

Prayer

Today be open to someone's love for you; let them take you into their heart.

O God, be our host, so we can be your guest. Be at home in our hearts, and send away all fear. Make our hearts quiet, forgiving, peaceful. When you have come into our hearts, take us into your own. Fill our lives with love. Amen.

Angel of Parties

Angels celebrate each person
with homemade angel cake.
One by one, come to the party,
Food and angels, come and take.

Right here, right here's an angel,
Right in this very spot,
If we believe it's so
Or if we think it's not.

Right here and now are angels,
They camp around our home,
And everything tastes better,
And we are not alone.

The young girl spoke softly to herself as she drew an angel party. A room filled with angels holding out flowers to boys and girls, and a cake with candles. Then she explained her picture to me: "Angels celebrate each person and meet them with a flower."

A party. That's where she meets her angels.

Wherever we are is a party when God's angels are with us. And there are angels right here—at dinner, at breakfast, at bedtime. Angels decorate the places where we are, to make us feel special, feel holy. God gives them gifts to bring to us. All kinds of angels make the party; it's what angels do.

Whenever candles are lit in church or our homes, whenever we pray, wherever we are, God is with us—right there! And so are God's angels. It's God's party time. Light a candle now as a reminder that God is with us and God's angels are, too. What a great reason for a party.

There is a right-here angel picture in King David's Old Testament songbook. Psalm 34, verse 7, says: "The angel of the Lord camps around those who fear him, and delivers them." That's happening where you are. Angels are making their camps all around you—to stay near you, to keep you safe. All you need to do is trust God (that's what "fearing" God means).

And then what happens? Everything tastes better! It's true. We can be so scared we don't feel like eating. Remember times you were so scared you didn't want to eat, or your food didn't taste good? Angels keep us safe and take away our fear. They make our food taste better. Everything tastes like party food.

And it's all happening right here, right now. Camps of angels. Parties of angels. So look for God's angels around you. Feel safe. Enjoy your food.

I wonder . . .

- ♥ how fast angels travel and how they get back and forth.
- ♥ if angels live wherever they are, or if they have a home someplace.
- ♥ what angels are doing right now, right near us.

What if . . .

- ♥ we saw someone today as an angel?
- ♥ we really believe an angel is beside us right now?
- ♥ we imagine angels being here now and talk about what they look like?

A party is . . .

- ♥ when you don't have to go anywhere else for something great to happen.
- ♥ when whatever you want to happen is already happening.
- ♥ when all the good places you'd like to be come together where you are.

Angel food to share

Make—or buy—and decorate an angel food cake together. Use colored icing, candy hearts and flowers, candles—whatever you want. Let each person decorate one section of the cake. Think about why it's called an angel food cake. Then eat the cake while you talk about the *I wonder* and *What if* questions together. How does your angel food cake taste when you know there's a camp of God's angels right beside you?

Prayer

Light candles to remind you of God's party when you pray together.

O God, thank you for your parties and for your promise to be with us to celebrate. Thank you for camps of your angels right here, right now, to keep us safe and to make our food taste better and to party with us. Thank you for making our life fun. Amen.

Angel of the Cross

The child drew an angel floating in the sky. Next to the angel, he drew a yellow star. He didn't know how to make the star's points just right. The more he tried, the heavier his star became. Finally he made the whole star thicker and longer. The star became a cross.

He brushed off the excess crayon and tilted his head as though to say: "That's just what I want it to be."

Do you remember looking into a light, squinting and seeing the light burst into stars? If I kept looking, the light turned into crosses and sunbursts. When I was little, I saw the altar candles in church that way. If I squeezed my eyes real hard, I would see crosses inside the candle lights.

Angels, a star, and a cross were all connected by the Christmas story. As Mary held her baby, surrounded by angel songs and the glow of the star, she must have felt great joy. But not long after this happy time, Mary was told that her child would one day suffer, and a "sword would pierce her own soul." For Mary, the image of the cross mingled with the star's glow and the angels' songs.

The star of Bethlehem reminds us, too, of the cross of Calvary. The cross within the star is the light that marks our Christmas celebrations. The Easter cross has become our Christmas gift.

I still look at light in different ways. If I squint a certain way, I can see a star around the golden cross above the altar at church. The cross expands into a star. Sometimes, in the brightness of the cross, I also see reflections of faces—my friends at church. I like to see all these together. And I know there are angels nearby, singing songs of joy.

There was a cross inside Mary's star. But it was still a star, with light and hope and promise. And there were angel songs of good news and joy.

I wonder ...

♡ what it means when I mark a cross on someone.
♡ why the cross looks like a plus sign.
♡ in how many places I can see the sign of a cross around me.

What if ...

♡ we hung crosses as decorations on a Christmas tree?
♡ I sometimes marked the cross on my forehead and felt special?
♡ we squinted at lights and told each other about crosses and stars we see?

A cross is ...

♡ when something is so heavy you can't hold it alone.
♡ good news and bad news on the same spot.
♡ a star marker Jesus left us.
♡ a light that no darkness can hide.

Star stickers of hope

Cut out small, colored stars, or buy a packet of gold foil stars. Whenever anyone is having a dark day, write a prayer for encouragement and help. Glue a star onto the prayer sheet and give it to the person: a reminder of the hope and light that Jesus brings to our dark times.

Prayer

Take something negative, hurting, and look at it in a positive way.

O God, this day show me a star around my cross. Make something good out of something sad. Lift me up when I feel down. You promise that nothing is too hard or heavy to carry. Put a star around our family, and let us all see the light you bring and hear your angels' songs of joy. Amen.

Angel of Honor

Sometimes I feel like standing,
Sometimes I bow so low;
Feeling very honored
I whisper soft, "Hello."

Sometimes I stand there looking,
With nothing I can say.
I feel so very honored:
God's angel passed my way.

She drew angels in all kinds of postures before God. God was in a cloud. Angels were bowing, flying, standing in a row, and one angel was saluting. Under the drawing she wrote: "Being before God." She kept on drawing angels. She knew what she must draw, and she added labels beneath each drawing: a tombstone surrounded by flowers was labeled "Grandma's grave"; a little girl standing with angels on a cloud, "A new girl comes to heaven"; an old woman flanked on one side by an angel and on the other, a crib filled with flowers, "An angel welcomes Grandma in heaven."

She wakened in me wonderful memories of honor. It felt good to stand up when Mrs. Heckel came into the room. Mrs. Heckel was older than my parents. I was little, but I felt what happens when you honor someone. It also felt good to kneel in church sometimes. Kneeling made those times special, and kneeling made me special. I felt God's honor flow through me.

Some Christians make the sign of the cross when Jesus' name is mentioned in church. When they make that sign in front of their faces, or mark it on their bodies, I feel honor in the air. The room becomes special, I am special, and all of us in the room are special.

Honor was in all the little girl's drawings. Young and old people were in heaven, surrounded by angels, bowing, bowing, bowing. Heaven is already a place of honor for the little artist.

The writer of the Gospel of Luke draws a picture of honor. An old man named Simeon came to the temple to honor God. Mary was also at the temple with her young baby, only a week old. She handed the child to the old man. Simeon took him in his arms and thanked God, saying: "Lord, you have kept your promise. I have seen your promised Savior. Now I may die in peace."

Old Simeon was honored by the child, and he showed honor to the child and to the God who kept his promise. We can feel honored by the old, or by the very young. Any age can be that special, and make us stand tall, or bow down.

To show honor, some people bow, some stand silent, some kneel, some stand at attention, some close their eyes. Honor has many shapes and forms. There is a very strong, good feeling about showing honor. It's something that even God's angels like to do.

I wonder ...

♡ how angels act when they honor God.
♡ what angels say when I honor and respect someone.
♡ how angels honor and welcome those who come to heaven.

What if ...

♡ we honored God in worship as angels do?
♡ we honored someone in the family as a surprise?
♡ we found a way to respect and honor older people?

Honor is ...

♡ when you feel special if someone comes into the room.
♡ when someone you know makes you feel speechless inside.
♡ when you feel greater because of something even greater than yourself.

Showing honor to God and to one another

Think of one new way—something you've never done before—to show honor to a person in your family, to an older person in your neighborhood, to a young child you know, and to God. Then do each of those things during the next week.

Prayer

Imagine ways to honor each other.

O God, you have honored us each with life; we will honor you with our life together. You have given us each a spirit of love; we honor you in our love for our family. You have given us heroes; we will be heroes to someone else. O God, you have honored us, and we thank you. Amen.

Angel of Love

*God wrapped the earth
in the heart of heaven:
That's what happened
on God's Day Seven.*

*God's angel of love
gives peace on earth.
God's hug gives the world
a second birth.*

One little boy drew heaven all around a big, round world, and an angel hugging the world. Then he drew Jesus in the center of the world. He said, "That's the world on Sunday."

Who could say more about God's love than the boy imagined in that one drawing? God's love is holding our earth close, and Jesus is with us. A wonderful Sunday.

Jesus came to bring peace, love, and rest. The story of Jesus is part of the old story of God—a story of love. It began in the very beginning, when God created everything. Each day of creation was an act of love. Then God blessed everything with a day of rest. God wished the earth peace, rest, love.

The day of Jesus' birth and Easter Day can both be seen as a second Seventh Day, a day of peace, rest, and love. These are big celebrations to remind us how much God loves us.

And each Sunday is a small celebration of that love. God keeps renewing his creation through the day of peace, rest, and love.

The child was right to draw an angel hugging the world. It is a picture of God's love through God's messengers of love. Holding and hugging are wonderful ways of loving.

Today a mother I know brought her firstborn child to my office. Her baby was in a basket, sleeping under a soft quilt. She lifted the child into her arms, removed the quilt, and showed me the little girl. I watched the mother looking down at the child in her arms. It was a look of love. Never before had I seen the woman with such a Sunday look, a look of peace and rest, a mother's look. To me she looked a lot like God must have on the seventh day of rest.

The boy's drawing pictured heaven all around the world. Not just above, but all around. In that heaven was God's angel with its arms surrounding the world. And, in the middle of the world, there was Jesus—the center of our world, the center of our lives. "That's the world on Sunday."

With God's love hugging us close and Jesus at the center of our lives, every day is Sunday.

I wonder . . .

- ♡ how God's angels keep loving when there's so much hurt on earth.
- ♡ how angels like to spend Sunday, the day of rest.
- ♡ what angels do during a worship service.

What if . . .

- ♡ we could see angels bringing love to us?
- ♡ we saw people acting as loving angels?
- ♡ we saw the whole earth held together by angels with God's love?
- ♡ I saw my life through the eyes of an angel of love?

Love is . . .

- ♡ when I get hugged so it leaves fingerprints on my mind.
- ♡ when I look at someone in a way that our hearts have the same beat.
- ♡ what God gives us to keep forever by giving it away to others.
- ♡ the reason God makes things live.

Sundays of love

Make Sundays—or any day—extra special by doing loving things for people close to you. Hug a friend. Rock a baby and sing to it. Give your dad or mom a backrub. Kiss your brother or sister on the cheek. Shake hands with someone you don't know.

Prayer

Hold or touch someone in a restful, peaceful, loving way.

O God, help us to know how dearly you hold us from every side. You hold us from inside so we feel good. You hold us from beneath so we feel safe. You hold us from above so we feel wanted. You hold us from all around so we feel saved. Thank you for this love. Amen.

Angel of Mercy

Angels fly with headsets,
music fills their ears.
They're on their way to worship
through glory glory spheres.

Angels fly with headsets,
they know the hills, the seas,
the streets and city alleys;
they fly with bumblebees.

They know the sounds of praises,
they hear the cries of need;
they care for those who suffer;
and answer prayers with speed.

A boy drew angels wearing headsets. His angels were in touch with each other throughout the universe. Headsets were their connection with each other and with God. When he finished his drawing, he smiled and held it up for me to see. He liked what he drew; he liked what he was thinking and feeling about angels.

A child drew angels with headsets. I thought the picture was unusual. Months later, I went to a funeral. On the table with the guest book were photos of the deceased. Many of these showed him wearing a headset. In his life, he talked to the whole world through ham radio. The minister, who was also into ham radio and headsets, gave the sermon. He spoke about the dead man's hobby. Both men got to know one another through their headsets.

I thought of the child's drawing: angels with headsets.

The minister told how, while wearing headsets, they sang, prayed, talked of God, listened to one another's worries and joys, talked about how they could help people in need. They showed mercy through their headsets. They spoke through sound waves of angels. So I believe some angels do wear headsets to show God's mercy. Being in touch with the world—in whatever way—is an act of mercy, and mercy takes angels to do it.

Mercy is an old word to describe God. It means "compassion," caring about others. The rainbow is, for many, God's sign of mercy in the sky. The rainbow is a code for "mercy" that we can read, even as ham operators read dots and dashes.

Mercy means goodness and love, too. Another sign of God's mercy came as a child wrapped in swaddling cloth. Mercy was also an innocent, good man dying on a cross. These are all signs of God's mercy to us.

Angels of mercy take many forms. We see them in all colors, shapes and sizes. Signs of God's mercy travel through the universe like sound waves, which many hear on headsets, in all kinds of languages. But signs of mercy don't need headsets to be heard; they are in the world all around us. These signs are real in our neighborhoods, and they are real in our families; we can hear them if we listen with the ears of angels.

I wonder . . .

- ♡ how many ways there are to show mercy.
- ♡ what's the hardest kind of kindness there is.
- ♡ how merciful our family is.

What if . . .

- ♡ there was no word at all for hate, just words for mercy and kindness?
- ♡ all enemies were kind to one another for one day?
- ♡ you could hear the rainbow talk about God's mercy?
- ♡ all sound waves carried songs of goodness and mercy for a week?
- ♡ there were a department of mercy in every state?

Mercy is . . .

- ♡ listening to someone so you can hear what they feel.
- ♡ feeling what it's too hard to say.
- ♡ looking all around for the person who's hurting.
- ♡ having medicine in your eyes when you talk.

Listening with mercy

Try an exercise in mercy. Sit down with a family member, or call a friend on the phone, and really listen to them. If you're sitting with them, listen with your eyes, too. Don't talk about yourself. Don't give advice. Ask questions, if you need to. Mostly, listen. How are they feeling? What do they need? What are they happy about? After you've listened, tell them thanks.

Prayer

See a sign in nature that is for you a symbol for mercy.

O God, I believe you forgive my sins and you give me your mercy. Cheer me up by helping me see how much you care about me. Cover me with mercy to guard me. Surround me with mercy to free me. Fill me with mercy to satisfy me. Hold me with mercy to save me. Amen.

Angel of Believing

Three good angels in a row,
Heaven comes to earth;
Three keep watch
where wise men go,
Marching to the birth.

Three good angels,
hearts of green,
Silent in a row;
Ah, the wonder they have seen
Only saints can know.

The girl was seven years old. She drew three angels for the three Christmas kings. The angels were greater and taller than the kings. That was amazing. And, more wonderful, she gave each angel a green heart. Under the picture she printed: "Heaven comes to earth, and three angels come to earth, each has a green heart."

The thought came to me, "These are angels of believers."

All week long, I talked with two hundred children about angels, the earth, and God. One girl put these things together in a special way. She drew three angels with the Christmas kings—one angel to watch over each king—and she gave the angels green hearts.

There was something about these kings, she knew, that would give their angels green hearts.

Adults might have given the kings' angels purple hearts for courage and bravery. The kings had traveled a long, hard time to find the newborn Jesus. And they had disobeyed wicked King Herod by not telling him where the baby was. All that took courage. Perhaps these brave kings even helped to save the life of the child. They were heroes of faith, heroes of believers.

The girl didn't say why the kings' angels had green hearts, so I can only guess what she thought. Maybe it was because their kings were like new. They had met the baby Jesus, and their hearts were made fresh and new, like springtime.

Or maybe that's just what *I'd* like the angels' green hearts to mean. It's a nice thought.

I wish I had asked the girl what the angels and kings were hearing, for in her drawing the kings looked so silent. They had no mouths. We have all been to visit a place or a person so special that there was nothing we could say. We are struck silent. We leave silently, on tiptoe, believing wonderful new things. Our voices grow softer as we go on our way believing.

She also printed these words under her drawing: "Heaven comes to earth." There is a beautiful Christmas hymn that has similar words: "From Heaven Above to Earth I Come." Now whenever I sing this hymn, I see angels with green hearts and the kings they watched over. And I see a little girl being glad while drawing green hearts inside the angels.

I wonder . . .

♡ how my believing began.
♡ if hugging someone helps them to believe.
♡ if believing begins when a baby is being loved.
♡ if God sometimes uses an angel to help me believe.

What if . . .

♡ we phoned a believer we know and thanked them for believing?
♡ I read something Jesus said, and believed it is especially true for me?
♡ I believed something with someone else?
♡ we told each other what's hard to believe while we held hands?
♡ we practiced believing by closing our eyes and trusting?

Believing is . . .

♡ how I know spring follows winter.
♡ when I look for a flower bud to open.
♡ why we can sleep in a storm.
♡ when a miracle picks us up and carries us.

My angel of believing

Draw and color a picture of the angel God sends to help you believe. What color will you make its heart? Will it be singing or quiet? Talk about your angels of believing together.

Prayer

Describe a believing angel.

O God, I believe. Help me when I do not believe, or do not believe enough. Hold me when I worry. Hold me when I am afraid. Hold me when I need to feel something brave. Hold me when I need to believe. And make my heart new and green like springtime. Amen.

Angel of On High

A child drew a picture of angels coloring the sky. Blue, red, gold—all the brightest colors in the box. But she colored only the top part of her paper. I asked her why. She said, "The angels are coloring God's home. God lives on high." Someone had taught her one name for God in the Bible, "The Most High One."

The girl said: "God lives on high." This reminded me of when I was young in a rural church. The ceiling in our country church was painted a light blue. Metallic patterns broke up the color so it looked like the sky. I always thought the sky was the ceiling of our church. Even though I felt God closest in the people around me, in the flowers and trees of his world, and especially in the Bible that lay open in the pulpit, I still liked looking up as though God were on high. "High" was past the ceiling of the church and past the ceiling of the sky.

The singers and poets in the Bible wrote about God as the High One, the Lifted-Up One, the Greatest. Although I know that God is also down among us, between us, and inside us, I love those pictures of God being On High.

When I think of God as close, like a good friend, or nearby in the people around me, I say "you" in my prayers to God. When I think of God as being beyond the stars and planets, beyond the highest heaven, I want to say "Thou."

I knew a woman who prayed "Thee" and "Thou" to God when she prayed aloud. I am sure that, at the end of her ninety-five years, when she was praying silently in bed, she prayed "you." But when she prayed aloud, she sat upright and focused her whole being toward the High God. Then she spoke with honor, distinctly, using her best grammar and her finest voice. When she prayed that way, she looked elegant. She looked the same way she felt about God: High.

In many Old Testament prophecies, royal and noble images were used to describe the Messiah who would come. People watched for him in castles, palaces, and high places. Then God came from On High, into a manger. He took up carpentry and lived without even owning a house. When Jesus was thirty-three, he was killed. Then he came back to life and was lifted up On High. God is On High. God is with us.

I am glad the child's drawing had bright colors when picturing God's home On High. It's not hard to imagine angels with paintbrushes mixing up the brightest colors to decorate God's home On High.

I wonder ...

♡ how high is "On High."
♡ if angels can fly faster the higher they go.
♡ if "On High" could ever be inside a person.
♡ whether "On High" is like being on a mountaintop.

What if ...

♡ we sometimes looked straight up to pray?
♡ we looked at the setting sun while thinking of God?
♡ we thought of God being very far and very near at the very same time?

On High is ...

♡ when I cannot go up any farther.
♡ higher than the top of a Ferris wheel.
♡ farther than outer space.
♡ the nearest anyone special can be to me.
♡ where I am closest to God.

Up high reminders of God

Put reminders of God in places that will make you look up. Make or cut out colorful pictures of angels. In large, bold letters, print names for God ("High One," "Lifted-Up One," "Most High God," "Lord," "Jesus," "Savior"). Then place the angel and name reminders above doors, on the ceiling above your bed, over the mirror in the bathroom—places that will lift your eyes above the worries and cares of the day, so you're reminded of the awesome God who loves you.

Prayer

Think of God in the finest, highest, most noble way you can.

O God, help us to see Thee as beyond us, as far greater than us, as the Highest there is. Help us often to speak to Thee in a special way, to feel Thee as special.

Help us also to see you as being here with us. You are holy, and still you were born in this earth, lived a life like one of us, in order to make us special. Thank you, O God On High. Amen.

Angel of Wonderful

One of the youngest boys drew an angel with very large eyes. The eyes were larger than the wings. He named it "Wonderful." Just the right name for an angel with huge eyes. An angel who has seen so much of God and God's love. An angel who is filled up with wonders, full of wonder.

Wonderful. What a playful word. Wonder-full. Full of wonder. Imagine being full of wonder that stays in you, like a name. Imagine being filled with wonderful thoughts and feelings, with sights and sounds of beauty, paintings, music. Imagine going somewhere that people say is "wonderful." In the Old Testament, a preacher said that the promised Savior—Jesus—should be called "Wonderful." Isn't that a perfect name for Jesus?

There are so many things in God's world that can fill us with wonder. To me, distance is wonderful, close-up and far-off distance. I feel the wonder of distance when watching news on television, when turning a globe of the world, flying on trips, phoning a friend, sending e-mail on my computer. Distance was a wonderful idea to me as a child—space between places. I was amazed by distance.

One of my favorite times in my childhood church in Pickrell, Nebraska, was when we broke bread in Holy Communion. I believed it was wonderful because when we broke bread, we were connected with Christians of all times, all around the world. In that moment, we were in a million different places at the same time, without ever leaving our little church in Nebraska. Talk about wonderful!

I believe that angels know and feel this wonder of distance. They travel faster than any imaginable speed and cover enormous distances in a flash. Think of all the Bible stories about angels: they suddenly appear out of nowhere. Think of the distance they cover without making a sound. That's just one reason why angels must be filled up with wonder.

And think of the wonders that angels have seen. The night above Bethlehem was filled with glory songs of wonder as angels watched the birth of the baby called Wonderful. Angels at the open Easter grave announced the wonderful truth they had seen: "He is risen."

Wonderful. The right name for an angel. The right word for all of us who have seen God's love. Imagine holding that wonder inside until it becomes part of us, like a angel's name.

I wonder . . .

- ♥ if I fill up with wonder when I'm wonderful.
- ♥ if being filled with wonder makes us heavier or lighter.
- ♥ why something wonderful makes me cheer and shout.
- ♥ in what part of my body I feel wonder fastest.

What if . . .

- ♥ my name was "Wonderful"?
- ♥ we named something "Wonderful" and treated it that way?
- ♥ I looked at someone until I saw them as wonderful?
- ♥ we named the five most wonderful gifts from God?

Wonderful is . . .

- ♥ when your eyes are filled with something beautiful.
- ♥ a miracle happening inside another miracle.
- ♥ a name for Jesus when I run out of all other names.
- ♥ something I can't ever afford and get to keep forever.

A bot full of wonders

Carry a pad of paper and a pencil with you for one week. Look and listen for wonderful things and wonderful people you meet. Write each wonder down on paper and put it in a box. At the end of the week, open the box and talk about the wonders you have collected. As you fill up with the memories of those wonders, say a prayer of thanks.

Prayer

Think how your life is full of wonders to share.

O God, fill me up with wonder. Help me to count my many, many blessings. Let me add them up so I know the gifts I have. Help me be more thankful so I enjoy more what you give me. Show me that when I am overflowing with gifts, I can give to family, to friends, to strangers. O God, focus my heart now on what is wonderful far-off, and what is wonderful very near to me. Amen.

Angel of Peace

*Sometimes lions honor God
with a deep and mighty roar.
If they had angels on their backs,
then lions might roar more.*

*Now might it be that animals
who roar, meow, and sing,
Give praise to God
in their own ways,
their worship to their king?*

Two hundred children drew angels for me to see. Many of the younger children also drew animals with wings—angel transportation. No animal was wild in their drawings. Lions, giraffes, and dolphins carried angels proudly over forests and seas.

When angels sang God's peace on earth, they gave God's peace to the whole earth. Peace is for every living thing.

I liked animals as I grew up. Some animals were pets. Many we called "wild." I studied their pictures and memorized their footprints in magazines and in the snow. I learned their trails and their calls. I watched for them. They were beautiful, doing what God made them to do. They seemed so peaceful, even though we called them wild.

I wished not to fear them. I tried to understand their lives and habits. They seemed like members of one great family with me. This was a community larger than the Brokering family; this was God's family. That thought drove away my fear of animals.

Fear can make something tame seem wild. Fear can make a friend an enemy. War comes from fear. What we don't understand, we often fear. War comes when we see the other person as foreigner or stranger, as wild. God created us for peace.

I love the creation story in Genesis, with its refrain after each day of God's creation: "And God saw that it was very good." Everything created fit together, everything was at peace. All of creation was one family.

God says we are to have dominion over creation, over the birds of the air, the fish of the sea, over all creatures on God's earth. Dominion means lordship. We are to treat dolphins and doves and canaries as a lord would, as a queen would—as ones who love and honor everything in their kingdom.

No wonder animals appear in the Nativity story. No wonder artists have painted doves into the rafters of the stable. Birds and beasts shared the stable with angels of peace. I believe that, if the shepherds heard the angel song, so did their flocks of sheep. Peace fell upon the whole world.

When I was little I believed animals praised God. I want to believe that again. Sometimes, when I stand quiet, I hear every living thing singing on earth, in the sea, from the sky, giving glory to God. A world of peace.

I wonder . . .

- ♡ what animals feel like when they're mistreated.
- ♡ when an animal is most happy.
- ♡ if animals make sounds that feel to them like singing.
- ♡ what we could learn from animals about peace.

What if . . .

- ♡ you could ask an animal a question about God?
- ♡ animals could say a prayer?
- ♡ an animal could tell us their language?
- ♡ there were a hymn that all beasts and birds sing at once?

Peace is . . .

- ♡ respecting another creature's space.
- ♡ having no fear.
- ♡ believing the world is one family.
- ♡ being a relative to a lion and a lamb at once.

Angel fun

In your mind, make a halo and wings for one animal you know. See the animal as part of your family. What animal will it be? How can you share peace with that animal? How can it teach you about sharing peace with your family? With your neighborhood? With the whole world?

Prayer

See an animal as created by God, as part of your family.

O God, thank you for the world of animals that roar and run and play and sing to you. You made them for us to know and to love. Through them, you bring us healing and joy. In them we see your beauty and spirit. Help us create a family of peace in the universe you have made. May your peace, O God, be in us, through us, and between us. Amen.

Angel of Safety

God, send me your safety angels.

Angel wings
are like a shield,
A fortress 'round my bed,
Helmets made
of brightest light,
Protecting heart and head.
Stronger still
and safer far
Than weapons,
shield, and sword,
Who come at night,
in quiet dreams,
And whisper
God's strong word.

Some children drew angels of safety. The children all knew about the school safety patrol. Their angels stood on street corners. Their wings were so wide they stretched off each side of the page. No one would cross the path of these angels without permission, without first making sure the street was safe.

Their drawings made me feel safe, as I did when I was little and prayed about angels guarding my bed. So I wrote a prayer about safety angels.

When I was five, I crawled far out on a limb of our mulberry tree to pick the ripest fruit. Going that far out and feeling the limb bend was fun. But when I couldn't get back to the trunk, fun turned to tears. I did not cry for long. There came my mother with the ladder. I was safe again.

I especially like feeling safe in the night. There is a night prayer I have always known by heart. I don't remember a time when I didn't say that prayer at bedtime. In the prayer, armies of angels surround my bed, shielding me with weapons against Satan. And they stay all night long. For seventy years, this angel army has been a protection. God keeps us safe longer than seventy years.

I like the safety angels in the Bible. Often these weren't armies of angels; they worked by themselves. Think of the angel in the fiery furnace with three men who wouldn't bow down to an idol. Those men walked out of that furnace without even smelling like smoke. And think of the safety angel who closed the mouths of hungry lions so they wouldn't eat Daniel.

I like the New Testament angel who warned Joseph about King Herod's plan to kill baby Jesus. In a dream, Joseph heard that angel of safety and believed the warning. Baby Jesus was saved from the wicked king.

When I was little, my family had safety angels all around. When I grew up and had my own family, I felt these angels all around us, too. I felt safe in the house: safe in our kitchen as we ate, safe in the evenings when we told favorite Bible stories, safe at night when we listened to prayers. The safety angels become more real when prayers are shared and stories of God are told and believed by father, mother, children, and friends. Then everyone feels safe and peaceful.

God's angels of safety are armies around my bed and street-corner guards with wings that stretch out of sight. No wonder the children drew their angels so large.

I wonder . . .

♡: what makes angels so strong.
♡: why I sleep better when I feel safe.
♡: what my safety angel does while I sleep.

What if . . .

♡: we had adult safety patrols of angels?
♡: we looked at our family as being safety angels to each other?
♡: there was a department of safety angels in the government?

Safety is . . .

♡: being held when you go out on a limb.
♡: knowing you're safe even when you can't see how.
♡: believing someone who loves you is always near.
♡: a bungee rope that never, ever breaks.

A safety poem

Listen and draw what you see on paper, in the air, or in your imagination.

Safety angel, wide and long,
Sing to me a safety song.
When I'm hanging in midair,
Bring a ladder or a chair.
When I wander or I roam,
Spread your wings and take me home.
Spread your love from left to right
'Round this day and through tonight.

Prayer

Make someone feel safe and strong today by what you do or say to them.

O God, awaken a feeling of safety in me, a feeling of your loving presence that makes me happy and strong. Grow that feeling in me, so I believe that you will never, ever leave me. And through me and my family, help others feel your strength and your safety. Make the story of my life strong and safe, for myself and for those around me. Amen.

Angel of Seed

Two children worked together on their drawings, checking what the other was adding, talking about the pictures they were making. They drew angels as farmers. One angel was sowing seed in a green field. The other was picking ripe fruit from trees. So quickly did they show me the two ends of life: new seed ready to be planted, old seed ready to be harvested. Both tended by angels.

When I was very young I planted seed into empty eggshells, set them on a sunny, winter windowsill, and watched them sprout and grow with drops of water and with light. A miracle. I felt the miracle of the seed inside me.

The seed was old and new at the same time. Seed is both ends of the miracle called life: it is old, the harvest picked; it is new, the beginnings of life.

I am like seed. I am old, the harvest of my father and mother. I am new, the father of my own children. All of us are like this. We come into the world new, as babies from our parents; and at the same time, we carry inside us the possibility to create new babies, to pass on the history of our families.

This is a miracle. The family tree is a miracle. Think of it: from parents to children to grandchildren, we pass along pieces of our family. Texture of skin, color of eyes, moods of the spirit, height and weight, smile lines, freckles, dimples are passed on from generation to generation. That is how the human seed works. It is the same with tomatoes and corn and wheat. The past goes on into the future.

In order to sprout and grow and blossom, seeds need tending with good soil, rain, and sunlight. In the same way, we need careful tending to grow and blossom. Children and adults need homes filled with love. We need to be held and cared for, even as seed needs to be held and nourished in mother earth.

Two children drew angels as farmers: one sowing seed, the other picking fruit. Angels of seed, angels of life. We can become God's angels of seed to one another through the love we show, the prayers we share, the homes we build together. Then we are caring for the seed of life in each other, helping it grow and blossom and bear new seed.

The miracle of seed. Even when we die, part of us goes on living through our children. And from the beginning of our life on earth until its end, we are watched over and tended by God's angels.

I wonder . . .

- ♡ what the first seed was.
- ♡ how long a seed can last before going back in the ground.
- ♡ if angels have gardens.
- ♡ if I am a flower or a vegetable.

What if . . .

- ♡ a town grew a garden together?
- ♡ everyone gave seed and plants to each other in spring?
- ♡ we had a family garden, outside or in our house?
- ♡ we had a tree for a friend and we visited it?

Seed is . . .

- ♡ the smallest way to package life.
- ♡ what connects the past and the future.
- ♡ the thing that wants to grow in us.
- ♡ how God keeps life and creation alive.
- ♡ how God stores miracles in tiny spaces.

A family garden

Plant a garden from seeds and cuttings together. If the weather is right, plant outside; if not, make it a windowsill garden. One person can plant flowers; another, vegetables; someone else can grow green plants. Care for the garden together. Carefully watch for first signs of new life. Have a celebration when all the plants have sprouted.

Prayer

Think about the miracle of how you came to be who you are.

O God, like seed, keep us in your rain and give us plenty to drink. Keep us in your sun and grow us strong. Keep us in your earth and feed us well. Keep us in your love so we will never be sad. Keep us together so we will not be alone. Amen.

Angel of Brightness

I saw a little girl draw the gravestone of Justin, a friend who had died. Next to Justin's gravestone, she drew an angel holding a star. The little girl was six years old. She told me that the angel with the star will roll the stone away. Then she turned and drew another star at the top of the picture. "It's a light," she told me, "a star for Justin."

Sometimes I feel dark, gloomy, cold inside. Then something happens, and I suddenly feel light, bright, warm. That's how it seems inside myself, and others seem that way to me, too. An angel of brightness appears and sends the darkness away.

Angels of brightness sneak up on you, and suddenly they're there. And everything is bright. They bring stars with them.

I've always seen stars and light as wonderful, spectacular, mysterious—like God's angels. I look at light and think of angels. When I was growing up, I saw angel light in candles on the altar at my church, in a kerosene lantern in our barn, in the lighted wick turned low in my bedroom. Outside our country home, a bright yardlight flooded the darkness when we played tag at night. It seemed to make the moonlight dim. We loved to play in that bright light.

Even a small candle in the distance or a tiny star speck in the night seemed bright when I thought of it as angel light.

In later years, I saw this brightness in nurses who hurried through hospital hallways. They seemed to fly into darkened rooms, bringing light with them. I watched how they went. Another miracle was happening in the dark and quiet hospital. God was spreading light through angels of brightness.

Years ago, on the hills of Bethlehem, shepherds were blinded by wonderful angels of brightness. They shielded their eyes from the glowing skies. When shepherds saw the angel brightness, the Child of Light had been born in Bethlehem. Their dark night was shattered by light, brightness, warmth.

Angels of brightness come to chase away all kinds of darkness, to bring light and hope to our lives. They can appear in a burst of sky as angels sing, in the flashlight of a friend who finds us in the dark woods, in a candle glowing while our mother prays with us, in the star a little girl draws above her playmate's gravestone, in the eyes of a friend looking at us with love.

The child who drew the gravestone of Justin also added an angel of brightness—starlight for even the darkest night. There is so much brightness in God's love that angels reflect it everywhere.

I wonder ...

- ♡ if brightness is something we only see with our eyes.
- ♡ if I can see angels of brightness better with my eyes closed.
- ♡ if the brightness is God's glory that sticks to angels.
- ♡ when a family feels this brightness most.

What if ...

- ♡ one candle could be made to burn for a person's whole lifetime?
- ♡ we ate more often by candlelight?
- ♡ we held candles at a funeral and made a wish?
- ♡ we lit a candle to remember someone each day?
- ♡ we worshiped some night with flashlights?

Brightness is ...

- ♡ light that reflects off God.
- ♡ wiping away the dark.
- ♡ seeing through something into the other side.
- ♡ a light waiting to shine.

Flashlights and candles

Gather in a dark place with just one candle or a flashlight. Turn out all other lights. Talk about how you feel in the dark, how the light makes you feel. Then share your thoughts about the "I wonder," and "What if" sections above and read the prayer below.

Prayer

For one minute carefully look all around for an angel of brightness.

God, your miracles are faster than the eye; what we see is a light shining over what you have already done. We ask for something and you have already given it to us. Thank you for the angels who show us the miracles we receive from you. Thank you for the angels who chase away the darkness of our spirits. Shine on them so we see them even more clearly. And let us shine for one another. Amen.

Angel of Praise

Alleluia!
Angels fly with diamonds
and instruments of gold,
Know more sights of beauty
than people can behold.
Angels fly with music,
playing while they sing,
Singing alleluias,
blessing everything.
Alleluia!

The boy wasn't able to play the piano, the trumpet, or the violin. But he believed that angels like a good time with music. The sky he drew was full of angel musicians: some singing, some blowing horns, some beating on stars with drumsticks. One angel played a guitar with strings that looked very much like a spider web. His drawing was studded with diamonds. It was a glorious picture, so I wrote an Alleluia poem.

Alleluia. What a good word. Alleluia means "Praise God." Large choirs and orchestras can praise God. So can the soft, sweet strumming of a guitar. So can a spider spinning its web. So can a child drawing a sky full of angels with musical instruments. All are Alleluia-makers.

Alleluia. This tiny word gives peace and joy to so many people all over the world. It can be sung over and over, letting the praises pile up and spill out. Or it can stand all alone. Just the one word, Alleluia, can be a whole song.

There are other one-words songs of praise, too. In my travels, I visited a place called Buchenwald, a death camp where a minister was locked in a cement cell. Many other people were locked inside this camp, too. Each day the minister preached to them from the barred window of his tiny room. His sermon had to be short because, if the guards caught him, they beat him. His sermon was often only one sentence long.

He preached by lifting himself up to the tiny window. Holding onto the bars, he spoke to the hundreds of prisoners lined up outside for roll-call. In snow, rain, bitter cold, or burning sun, the prisoners were lined up outside. And each day, the minister spoke one sentence to them.

The prisoners who heard him were made strong by his words. Each day they waited to hear him preach again. Usually, he said just three words: "Jesus is Lord." That was enough to bless all the prisoners. That was a wonderful reminder, a simple Alleluia.

There are other simple sentences that express important truths, that say everything we need to know. "God loves me" can be enough to get us through a day. "I love you" can lift the spirits of someone who feels down. One kind word, one loving look from the eyes of another can do the same. These are simple Alleluias.

Angels praise God. That is their task. They can do it in choirs, with guitars, horns, and star-drums. We can praise God through our own Alleluias: a child's drawing of angels, a kind word to a friend, a sentence of hope through a cell window.

I wonder . . .

- ♥ how many ways there are to praise God.
- ♥ what would make our family feel like shouting Alleluia.
- ♥ why Alleluia is so much fun to sing.
- ♥ how we say thanks to God the best.

What if . . .

- ♥ all the world sang Alleluia at the very same time for one hour?
- ♥ we said Alleluia! when we were happy?
- ♥ some Sundays a sermon was one sentence long?
- ♥ we had a special family song we sang together?

Praise is . . .

- ♥ making your voice as glad as your heart.
- ♥ putting happy feelings on your lips.
- ♥ letting your heart fly like a kite.
- ♥ when you say thanks before it disappears.

Music of praise

Use music to praise God. Sing a favorite song together, or let each person sing one verse of his or her favorite hymn. Or play a tune on a musical instrument. Or play a hymn on a CD or tape and sing or hum along.

Prayer

Today, say a very good word or sentence that helps others.

O God, say a kind word to me, over and over. Tell me a true word or sentence I need to know. Say it in words, in music, in actions of others toward me. Let me hear a very good word or feeling for myself. And then let me say that good word to others. Help us keep your good word alive with one another. We praise you. Alleluia. Amen.

Angel of Joy

My angel's dressed in purple,
She's flying past the sun;
She's going to a party
Where angels have their fun.

A girl of six drew an angel named Emily who was going to a party. Emily is the name of her friend who died. The girl's angel had wings and a bright party dress and a ribbon in her hair. There was a kazoo in the picture, too. The little girl told me that there would be lots of other angels at the party with Emily.

I learned again that a friend can be an angel. So I wrote a poem about such an angel as Emily, an angel of joy.

A friend can be an angel. Emily, who had died and gone to heaven, had become such an angel. And, to her little friend, heaven was a party—with party dresses and hair ribbons and kazoos. What a happy picture: a party filled with angels of joy having fun.

Heaven has long been connected to joy, music, celebration, fun. For me, fun music means strings, country music, folk songs, jazz. For the little girl, it meant angels with kazoos.

I believe angels have fun, play musical instruments, not only in heaven, but on earth. In high school, I had a friend who played the saxophone and gave it a real angelic sound. At Christmas, I imagined hearing "Silent Night" played on the saxophone and on drums. Forty years later, I asked someone in a band to play "Silent Night" on the drums. He did, and it was great. At the funeral of my friend Jim, someone played "Amazing Grace" on a bagpipe. In a large women's convention, in honor of a friend, a minister came on stage and played "Beautiful Savior" on a musical saw. Sometimes the most unusual instruments can take on heavenly sounds and add fresh life and joy to old tunes. Surely those who love such music have something of God's joyful angels inside their souls.

I can still feel the joy I had when playing music on an empty oatmeal box, when I was five. I was a drummer back then, and I found joy in my instrument.

I believe angels of joy will play great golden horns at the next coming of Christ. Then we will all join Emily at the party in heaven. And if I could have my way, I would like Christ to come with drum rolls, a saxophone, a piccolo, and the humming of a cello. And, for Emily and her little friend, a kazoo as well. What a mix of joyful sounds to usher us into the party.

There are days that remind me of a party, filled with joyful sounds and angels sharing their joy. Some families find joy by celebrating tiny events each day.

So much in life is a party for God's people, and whenever they celebrate, the angels of joy are there, too.

I wonder . . .

- ♡ why having fun is also a medicine for the mind.
- ♡ why the Bible says that Jesus will come again to the sound of horns.
- ♡ what's the nicest angel music there is.
- ♡ why celebrating something in your life helps you remember it.

What if . . .

- ♡ we baked a cake for someone, and surprised them with it?
- ♡ our family baked a cake, with everybody helping to make it?
- ♡ we invited a musician to our house to make music with us?
- ♡ we formed a family band, using what we have at home, for fun?

Joy is . . .

- ♡ when laughter inside gets so great you can't hold it in.
- ♡ when you feel so good your face relaxes.
- ♡ something outside is so good you let it all come into yourself.
- ♡ when there are no walls or doors between people.
- ♡ when there's nothing to be afraid of.

A family band

Form a family band just for fun. Use "instruments" you find around the house—real instruments if you've got them and people can play them, or else use an oatmeal box for a drum, finger-snapping as castanets, water-glasses and spoons for chimes. Use your imagination. Then play a favorite tape or CD and join in with your family band!

Prayer

Listen for a musical sound that feels like a party.

O God, make something little into a celebration today. Help me raise up something so I like it and can remember it. Let your messengers of joy get to me and make me glad. Make me an angel of joy, to bring some beautiful word or tune to someone who needs to be made glad. Fill me up with good fun, and make me well. Amen.

Angel of Tears

She drew an angel crying. An angel of tears. She colored many, many tears. The bottom of the drawing was a sea of blue tears. The tears took up more space in the drawing than the whole angel. Her angel's eyes were closed while the tears poured down to the ground. The angel was crying, the little girl said, "because my baby brother is sick, and mommy's sad."

At this moment there are mothers and fathers and whole families weeping for how others hurt. Listen. There are tears, tears, tears in the world. People are sad and hurting because of sickness and anger and greed and because of the selfish, hurtful things others do to them. Do you hear the people crying?

God hears them crying and sees their tears, and God cries, too. And so do his angels. God is sad when we are sad or hurting.

What do we do when we read news of violence, and see the harm done against God's children? How do we comfort those who weep and mourn? I believe there are angels of tears, angels of comfort, who help us cry with those who hurt.

Two members of my family cry easily while watching news reports of violence—especially violence against children. They cry for those who hurt and for those who cause the hurt. They feel the pain, and they cry. Tears make a difference in how we see and hear the city news, how we see our world. There must be many angels of tears who look down, weep, cry, have pity, who know how it feels to hurt.

When I was little, I knew a minister who wrote songs about tears, love, human suffering, hurt. I sang along with his songs, and I cried along. Years later, I went with groups of people to visit camps of refugees who had lost their homes and friends. We saw great pain and sorrow in those camps. We joined our tears with those of the families and children in pain. We cried with them; and we also sang, shared food and clothing, smiled, talked, loved, felt sympathy. There were angels of tears in those camps.

Everywhere in the world there are angels who sing and who serve, angels who feel hurt and sorrow, angels who cry and bring comfort. We join those angels when we cry with those who are hurting. And we become God's angels of comfort whenever we do something loving to stop the hurting.

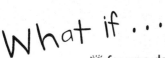

I wonder . . .

- ♡ how tears help us when we're sad.
- ♡ what made Jesus most sad.
- ♡ why people who are sad often look down.
- ♡ why being close to someone I love helps me when we cry.

What if . . .

- ♡ for one day no one hurt another person?
- ♡ we went to someone sad and stayed long enough to cry with them?
- ♡ we hugged each other when we felt like crying?

Tears are . . .

- ♡ for washing away disappointment and sadness.
- ♡ a way to know someone is hurting inside.
- ♡ what we do to share sadness and hurt.
- ♡ to wash our eyes so we can see clearly what hurts.

A prayer of tears

When you pray the prayer below, stand close together. Hold hands or put your arms around one another. Mention your own hurts to one another as you tell God about them. Pray for people you know—family, friends, neighbors, and others in the world—who are hurting. Cry with one another as you pray.

Prayer

Today I will notice something real causing someone to cry.

O God, let me feel the sadness of someone today. Let me be near them.

(Stop to add your own prayers for friends, neighbors, and others who are hurting. Tell God and each other about your own hurts.)

Help me find my tears if I have lost them, dear God. Help me accept others when they cry. Help me be with people when they need to find their tears, when they are very sad, or when they are glad. Help us express what is inside us, because you want us to tell you everything we feel. And help us remember how much you love us. Make us your special angels of tears to one another. Amen.

Angel of Glory Light

It was a child who introduced me to angels riding dinosaurs. She drew a tiny angel riding a great green dinosaur. Light radiated from the tiny angel and surrounded the earth all around the dinosaur. She colored the light yellow. What did the child mean to say? Perhaps she wanted to bring angels into her world of imagination. After all, why shouldn't God's angels be there, too? Or maybe she realized that angels have been around a long, long time—even back in prehistoric days. Or maybe she just wanted to picture the beautiful light that angels reflect to everything.

Picture this: an angel lighting up the earth around a dinosaur with glory. That's a lot of glory light.

In her drawing, the young girl decorated the road of the dinosaur with light. Imagine a tiny angel sitting on a dinosaur and radiating so much light that nearly the whole scene was bathed in yellow. That little angel and its enormous light touched even the world of dinosaurs. The drawing offered a wonderful picture of God's glory: the light of angels is reflected light, light that comes from being in the presence of God. And that's a lot of light. God's glory is a light that we, too, walk in. Imagine the angels around us who are casting light around us, lighting up the road on which we walk.

In an exciting story, a man named Saul walked into God's glory light. He was traveling to a town called Damascus. Suddenly his road was blazing with light. Saul fell to the ground and became a different person—a follower of Jesus named Paul. He met God in the light and, from that moment on, wherever he went, his road was lighted by God's glory.

A nine-year-old girl walked a dinosaur into the light of its own little angel, God's glory light. And, even though she may not have realized it, she was picturing the glorious journey of light that God's people have been walking since the beginning. From long before the time of dinosaurs, down to today, on into the future, God's light has shined and will keep on shining.

As she grows older, she will learn more stories of people walking in God's glory light. These are stories of a burning bush that marked the beginnings of freedom for God's people; of a pillar of fire guiding through the wilderness to a promised land; of a man who was the Way, the Truth, and the Light. It is one long, wonderful story that includes her own family, and yours.

I want that little girl's imagination. I want to see a stream of angels and glory through all history, flooding the earth in light. I want to to see God's glory light enveloping all cities, all nations, all races, and all angels. Light is a picture of God. And we are part of that picture, surrounded by angels of light.

I wonder . . .

- ♥ how much glory light there is in God.
- ♥ if God's light draws us to God like the sun draws a plant to it.
- ♥ where light goes at nighttime.
- ♥ if there is a glory light bulb inside the mind.
- ♥ why we think of glory light as yellow.

What if . . .

- ♥ glory light became our family symbol?
- ♥ we asked children to tell us about light?
- ♥ we asked the stars some very old questions about God?
- ♥ we thought about dinosaurs and God and angels being together?

Glory light is . . .

- ♥ when light is so bright you have to see the back of it.
- ♥ a light that shines when there is no other light.
- ♥ the inside of God's spirit made visible.
- ♥ a way to picture God without a face.

Glory light reminders

Make reminders of God's glory light, and use them during your devotions and prayer times. Pour about an inch and a half of sand in the bottoms of several clear or colored glass quart jars. Place a small votive candle on the sand in each jar. Light the candles for your family worship times. Sing songs about God's glory light, like "This Little Gospel Light of Mine" and "Pass It On."

Prayer

Look for signs of God's glory light in the people and things around you.

O God, your light is near to us. Walk with us in your light. Your light is around us even when we do not see the light. Thank you for all the light we know: the sun, the moon, electricity, candlelight. Thank you for the light we feel and see in each other, in the pictures of your angels, in the shining of our eyes. Thank you for the light we feel in a kind word, a kind touch, a kind feeling. Amen.

Angel of Birth

We gather 'round the little baby,
It's more than a new birth;
Inside this child so newborn
Are the gifts of God on earth.

A young boy hunched over his drawing in deep concentration. He drew a baby in a crib between a man and woman. To one side of the man was a young boy. The man and woman and boy had big smiles on their faces as they stood around the baby. This little family was in a basket held up by angels.

The boy had a new baby sister. This was his family. To this boy I give a poem.

I believed that an angel had delivered my older brother in a basket, and left him on the front porch of our parsonage. It was an awesome idea. Being born was a delivery from God.

When I was young, many of my relatives said I looked like my mother's father. Somehow in my birth, parts of grandpa got into me. Something from our family line—from our parents and grandparents and great-grandparents—stays alive in us. We inherit parts of how we look and who we are from our ancestors. And our family members see parts of themselves in us.

Jesus was from King David's family line. Jesus had royalty in his background, and some of that royalty was a part of him. Many, many years before he was born, God promised that, one day, a Savior would be born in the family that included King David. From birth to birth to birth, eager parents looked at their newborn babies with hope. This one, this one, this one could be the promised Savior. Imagine how excited people were every time a baby was born.

Being born puts us into a limelight. We are adored, admired, cooed over, examined in detail, protected like fine porcelain. A birth is a time for great hopes and expectations. There is so much possibility in each newborn baby. Could this child be the one who will make a great discovery, compose or play beautiful music, lead nations, show wisdom, become a great healer, bring peace on earth? That is what being born is about, being part of the family line and being something more. Wonderful possibilities.

Think of the even greater family each baby is part of. We are all children of God. What parts of God have been passed along to us? And what glorious possibilities are there for a child of God to become? Imagine the hopes and expectations that God has for each of us.

When I was little I believed my brother was brought from God. Now I know that we all are. No wonder God's angels watch over the birth of each baby!

I wonder . . .

- ♡ if being born is the greatest birthday in my life.
- ♡ how many ways my family is alive in me.
- ♡ which relatives gave me my kind of spirit.
- ♡ what happened in the world the day I was born.
- ♡ which parts of God I have inside me.

What if . . .

- ♡ all babies could live up to their best possibilities?
- ♡ each of us could live up to God's hopes for us?
- ♡ every baby could have their name inscribed on a memorial stone?
- ♡ I could give my best trait to the future?

Being born is . . .

- ♡ God making something alive from inside out.
- ♡ a way to see yourself in someone else.
- ♡ how we and God get to be relatives.
- ♡ how God honors us.
- ♡ the most wonderful present God gives.

The day you were born

Find out what happened on the day you were born, or at least in the year you were born. Talk with your parents, relatives, older friends and neighbors; check old newspapers in the library. Also talk with your parents and older brothers and sisters about their hopes for you. What did each of them hope and wonder as they held you when you were tiny?

Prayer

Hear a story about a birth and marvel.

O God, what did you mean to say by being born yourself in a manger in Bethlehem? I thank you for the gift of birth, that I might have this life, know your world, enjoy the earth, be in a family. Thank you the gifts I have inside me from families who came before me, for the talents and treasures of many kinds. Thank you for the gifts that come from being part of your family—love, kindness, forgiveness. Help me use my gifts to make a better life for myself and those around me. Forgive me when I fail. May each of my days be like a new birth, a new life, a new chance to live up to your gifts. Amen.

Angel of Royal

Angels, angels—all kinds of angels. For five days, children drew angels of every imaginable kind. As they finished, they called me over to show their pictures. Many colored their angels purple. Some wore crowns or carried crowns. Some were strong and had muscles like Atlas. Many of the angels were singing. Most were busy doing good deeds: watching over children, holding babies, carrying food.

Angels in purple with crowns, angels singing, angels doing good deeds. A nice collection of angels.

Jesus was royal, the Son of God and a member of King David's family, and he served others. He was a king and he washed his friends' feet. Imagine! I learned this about Jesus when I was little, and I liked this kind of king. That is also when I learned about angels who serve God by watching over us.

And there are angels who sing. The Christmas story tells us about them. Royal visitors to earth who sang wonderful news.

So I learned that royalty serves and sings. Throughout my childhood, I had these two kinds of angels in mind: those who served, those who sang. Some came with towels, some flew with hymnals. That's what angels looked like to me.

I knew people in our country church who were like those angels. Mr. Spilker served a lot, but I never saw him sing. I wondered if it was his voice or if he liked the serving angels more than the singing ones. I thought my father was both. He sang louder than the whole congregation, and he was good at making sick calls, at harvesting wheat with farmers, and at helping build things.

Mr. Hofling made us feel special when he came to the house to talk. He came in coveralls, dusty from the field, from working—a serving angel. But he also had singing-angel qualities. He told stories and laughed, and he smiled a lot, even though his daughter had polio. He didn't sing, but he painted pictures of joy in my mind. I believe he knew both kinds of angels.

It feels especially good to me when an angel sings while serving. My mother sang when she cared for me. Many people hum a tune when they rock babies. When I sing and serve at the same time, I really have God's angel of royal inside me.

My pastor wears a stole around his neck. The stole looks like a long towel to me. He could put it over his arm and serve me like a waiter. I look at him that way. He's a servant angel. When my pastor leads in worship and we all sing, I hear angels singing.

My church is full of purple angels, with towels and song-books. They help us feel we are royal, like queens and kings.

I wonder . . .

♥ what kings and queens like best to wear.
♥ why purple and blue are royal colors.
♥ who makes me feel royal and special.

What if . . .

♥ I lived in a royal palace?
♥ a prince or princess came to our house to visit?
♥ God came to us dressed as someone we know?
♥ God appeared to us as someone very poor?

Royal is . . .

♥ when a dandelion is treated like a rose.
♥ what makes anyone special.
♥ how you are to treat everything God made.
♥ singing while helping others.

Royal promise

Think of ways you could serve others—family, friends, neighbors. Make up a promise coupon ("Good for one hug," "I promise to dry the dinner dishes," "I will shine your shoes," "Two games of catch") for each person. Print it on purple paper, if you can. Hand these to the people you will serve. As you serve, how about singing a song?

Prayer

Look for persons who serve you, and those who make you glad with music today.

O God, give me a good towel for serving, and a good song to sing. Show me the fun of doing good to others. Help me to receive kindness from my family and friends. Put music into my mind so that I enjoy my work and play. O God, send me an angel, some kind of messenger, to make me feel royal, as you say I am. Amen.

Angel of Welcome

To a world of war and fighting,
In the center of the earth
Where the battles were terrific,
Came the silent little birth.
Welcome.

In the midst of all the danger,
Stands an angel at attention,
Near the baby in the manger:
A new member of creation.
Welcome.

The children worried about war. They drew many, many pictures of angels repairing the destruction of war: bombed cities, wounded soldiers, broken buildings, torn-down trees. Many of the angels were standing between soldiers, saying things like: "No more fighting," or "Now behave."

While those around him were drawing war scenes, one child drew the Christmas manger, the shed, animals, Mary, Joseph, the baby. From this nativity scene, a road stretched down to the bottom of the paper. On the road stood an angel holding a big sign that said "Welcome."

I'm sure the little boy meant his "Welcome" sign as a greeting for baby Jesus. But there's another kind of welcome in the nativity, too. I think Jesus came to be God's "Welcome" sign. Angels announced "Welcome" as they invited shepherds to visit the newborn Savior. And the birth of Jesus is also God's "Welcome" to us, showing us how much we are loved, inviting us to come to him.

Among all the pictures of angels repairing war and destruction, a little boy drew an angel of welcome at Jesus' birth. A picture of safety and peace and welcome.

What a wonderful feeling, to be welcome. When I was in college, away from home, I knew a family whose door was never locked. I loved going there, opening the door a little, and calling in: "Hello." There was always the same answer: "Welcome! Come on in." The place was like home. It was a warm, loving spot where I could get away from worries and pressures of college life.

Years later, someone gave me a doormat with the word "Welcome" molded in rubber. I laid it in front of the door to my writing shed in the woods. This was a private place, a place where I could find peace to think and write. Few others went there, or saw that welcome sign. But I saw it. Whenever I went to write in that little shed under the oak trees, I was greeted with a "Welcome." And I felt better.

In the little town of Bethlehem, nearly 2000 years ago, Jesus was born. Angels of welcome were posted to sing of that birth, to invite shepherds to the Prince of Peace. A place of welcome and safety, a place of peace.

Because of that birth in Bethlehem, we have a place of peace, too. Even in war and danger, God is with us. Good angels keep God's mat swept clean so we can always see the word: "Welcome."

Underfoot, just where you are right now, look for the sign: "Welcome."

I wonder . . .

♡ where angels of welcome are posted in our home.
♡ if we are a welcoming family.
♡ where I feel most welcome.
♡ what the best way is to make someone welcome.

What if . . .

♡ our family welcomed a new person into our home each week?
♡ every church had a bed and breakfast guest house?
♡ a guest room was required in every house?
♡ we celebrated a Welcome Sunday each year?

Welcome is . . .

♡ to wave before you even think about it.
♡ to feel at home away from home.
♡ knowing you belong where you are.
♡ hugging someone before they even get there.

Welcome exercise

Invite someone you don't know or don't know well to one of the following: a dinner at your home, a special church service, to join you for one of these devotions, a walk through the park, a cup of coffee and donuts.

Prayer

Be God's welcome sign today, for someone you've not really welcomed.

O God, in the middle of my traffic-filled life, open your door to me. Make the places I go your holy place. Be there to welcome me. Fill me with the peace and safety that come from your love. When I am in the middle of things, be there, too. Amen.

Angel of Blue

She drew blue angels on water skis, on the high seas. Their arms were outstretched, their hands lifted to the sky. Wings flowed out behind them like waves. The boy next to her had angels flying through the blue waters, sometimes riding the tips of white waves, high as mountaintops.

Angels having fun on water. Angels touching the sky.

Blue angels of sea and sky. I see angels of blue in places of water, in baptism waters, in springs and fountains born in mountains, on the Sea of Galilee. In such places as these look for angels of blue.

To me, blue is a color for angels. That is how children paint water and sky—deep blue. Blue is a strong color. The deep blue of sky or the deep blue of ocean: color of power and royalty, color of life. A good color for messengers of God.

The most royal blue for me is the Bethlehem sky, the night a baby was born in a stable. Angels of blue burst that sky with joyful news. When that baby grew up, he climbed mountains to share joyful news to people who followed him. His hands lifted to the sky, he preached words of power and life. Surely he was surrounded by angels of blue then.

When he climbed down from the mountains to the seaside, Jesus gave blind people back their sight and healed the lame, who took their bed mats and walked home. And once he stood in a ship inside a storm, stretched out his arms, and put the storm to sleep. Power and life. Angels of blue surely watched from the sky and the sea and danced for joy.

No wonder children drew God's angels in blue, skiing through the seas and waves, their wings brushing the sky.

Go in a boat, quietly, onto water, and you will find him there. Lean over a baptism font, watch the water, see the soul be quiet, and you will find him there. Look up into the blue heavens. He is there. And surrounding him are angels of blue, having fun, celebrating the life he gives.

In Jesus we find God's angels of blue.

I wonder . . .

- ♡ if angels swim under water.
- ♡ if angels can have both fins and wings.
- ♡ if angels climb mountains.
- ♡ if heaven has mountains and oceans.

What if . . .

- ♡ we pictured angels swimming in the sea?
- ♡ churches were ships?
- ♡ a congregation held its services on the sea or lakeshore?
- ♡ we worshiped God in a hot air balloon?

Blue is . . .

- ♡ the color of the sky you see in the water.
- ♡ a color that makes a baby feel peaceful.
- ♡ how a sky can look when it looks deep.
- ♡ the color of newborn eyes.

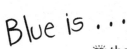

Worship in blue

Sit quietly beside a lake or river or sea; listen to the water and stare down at its power. Lie back on a hillside and stare at the spreading blue sky. Imagine these filled with God's angels of blue. Listen for the voice of God. Let your thoughts flow into a prayer.

Prayer

See yourself as member of God's most royal family of power and life.

O God, show me that I am special because I have your power and life inside me. Show me who I am deep inside. Show me that you want me here. Show me how I ride in your ship, on your high seas. Show me that you stand in my storms and quiet them. Show me that I am here for a royal reason to travel this way of life. Amen.

Angel of Hope

Angels come with candlelight,
Of tiny bits of fire.
Rockets shoot into the sky;
Candlelight shoots higher.

Angels know of warfare
that burns the air with fire,
And angels know a candle flame
that glows and burns still higher.

Of all the pictures the children drew, most had to do with hope. In their pictures, the children held out for a better world. Angels thwarted guns and fighter planes and bullets. Angels patched a wounded world and fixed broken forests. Angels cleaned lakes and oceans. The drawings were filled with candles and smiling angels. Children have a vision of hopefulness.

One drawing was of a fiery rocket in a war. But in the drawing, the child drew an angel with a candle that was bigger, and brighter, and burning higher than the rocket. So I was inspired to hope.

Sometimes older people's eyesight fades and they can't see well to read. At the same time, their eyes can look farther, see deeper, and imagine hope. Sometimes old persons and little children can see where hope comes from.

Eyes do grow dim. When the infant Jesus was taken to the temple, an old man named Simeon took the child into his arms. His eyes were almost blind, but in his heart he saw the child with twenty-twenty sight. He held the child and saw a light. He looked at the eight-day-old baby and spoke of glory. The opening words of his song were these: "God, you have kept your promise."

Rainbows appear in clouds. Light is bright when a cloud breaks open. Hope breaks through our storms and clouds like a fire. Suddenly we see clearly with our hearts.

In a dark sky, fire is especially spectacular. Fire can be a bolt of lightning, a falling star, showers of northern lights, a full moon, a slit of sunlight breaking through a storm. Or it can be holiday fireworks, a burst of colored flares, runway beacons.

Light spectacles make children shout for joy. Light suddenly shatters darkness and gloom: hope in the midst of war and destruction. We all need angels of hope carrying candles.

Deep inside children—inside us all—is a cloud of fear, fear of the war and violence we hear and see in the daily news. For hours, the children drew pictures of hope. Many drew angels stopping bullets, bending rifles, and pushing bullets back into guns. They want God's angels to do what is possible for God to do, to stop the hurts and killing and terror. They want God's angels to make things right.

God sends angels of hope to bring light to our dark and our fears. To see them, we need the eyes of children, both young and old—children of God who are angels of hope.

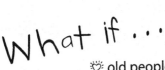

I wonder . . .

❤ what is the biggest enemy of hope.
❤ what our family hopes for most.
❤ what's the difference between wishing and hoping.
❤ if hope is tied to something it can count on.

What if . . .

❤ old people were hired to keep hope alive?
❤ Hope Day could be a national holiday?
❤ I carried an idea of hope with me each day?
❤ I prayed a prayer of hope when waking each
   morning?

Hope is . . .

❤ something impossible you can count on.
❤ believing without looking.
❤ leaning on something you can't see is there.
❤ a hidden miracle right under your eyes.

Candle of hope

Light a candle and gather around it quietly. As you stare into its light, tell one another your hopes—for yourself, for your family, for the world. Be bold. Hope for great things! By sharing hope, you build hope.

Prayer

Enjoy light today, such as the sun, a star, a candle, and make a wish.

O God, help us see candles and light as signs of hope in our home. Let us see what is not always easy to see, the goodness you give us each day. Help us look for what is close to us, that we often miss seeing. Show us what is far off, that you have promised us. Show us what you have done this day for us. O God, and let us be angels of hope to others. Amen.

Angel of Good News

A young boy drew an angel on a mission. The angel was carrying flowers through the sky. Down below was a little boy kneeling beside a sick dog. The boy was crying. Under the drawing, the artist wrote: "My agel is goig to heel a puppy. Jesus is glad. I like my picher."

The child liked his picture. His angel was going to heal a puppy. A good news angel with flowers. Good news for the puppy and the puppy's sad little master.

Children love good news. Good news can be words, it can be kind deeds, it can be flowers.

The boy wrote: "I like my picher." He liked what he drew, and what he liked had to do with Jesus. His picture of the angel with flowers was good news. The angel was on the way to heal a puppy, and that will make Jesus glad. Good news for everybody.

Children like to make things well with flowers. Flowers are good news: they heal, make us feel better, feel pretty, feel good. Why shouldn't angels bring flowers to a sick puppy?

When Spring comes and flowers grow, it's a good time. We say: "Come, see the tulips; they're blooming! The daffodils are open." It's time to make a homemade bouquet, to bring a violet to someone, to see a rose budding. When something lives, grows, blooms, it's good news. We feel better for such sights. They are God's gifts of healing.

It's great to find good news in the Bible, and it's great to find good news in the world around us. God sends good news in all kinds of ways, but we've got to open our eyes.

Look around you. There comes the sun, rising in the east, orange and fiery red, soft pink and lavender. Listen: hear the red-winged blackbird. Oh hear the oriole's song. Read about the sky in the book of Psalms, then see it out the window or walk outside with your eyes turned upward. God's good news again. God's good news is everywhere.

Sometimes we miss glad tidings, good news. Our eyes and ears are closed with worry. Then a good news angel comes along. Suddenly the sun begins to rise. A rainbow appears. The words of a good song pop into our minds. The whole world turns green in early spring. Autumn colors appear. We see full moons and night shadows. There are smiles meant just for us. Good news. We feel better.

Without our asking, God's angels of good news come. The young boy drew a good picture. Angels come to us with flowers, the sunrise, a tiny smile, a loving word, a hug. Good news angels keep coming.

I wonder . . .

- ❤ what's the most beautiful thing I saw today.
- ❤ what's the prettiest flower I know.
- ❤ what's the best good news in the Bible.
- ❤ what I'd like to see that I've never seen before.

What if . . .

- ❤ the newspaper printed only good news this week?
- ❤ we had a department of good news in the government?
- ❤ we took pictures of sunsets and saw them together?
- ❤ we recorded good news of our family in a diary or scrapbook?

Good news is . . .

- ❤ the title of God's book.
- ❤ words you want to think about when going to sleep.
- ❤ what makes your body happy.
- ❤ stronger than bad news.
- ❤ what dries tears.

Sharing good news

Give flowers to someone for no reason at all. Read a favorite Bible story together. Take someone for a walk to watch a sunrise or sunset. Smile at somebody and give them an unexpected hug.

Prayer

Let something beautiful reach out to you today.

O God, brighten my day. Make me glad with something beautiful today. Help me see the riches around me. Show me your creation, so I hear and see all the things near me that are mine to enjoy. Show me good news near me, far off, and inside me. Amen.

Angel of Behold

A nine-year-old girl drew an angel giving flowers to people leaving the earth for heaven. Some people were holding flowers as they flew up into clouds. They were all smiling.

The girl said, and slowly printed on her picture: "Each one who gets a flower gets to sit by Jesus. And see him up close." Then she drew many birds and flowers around the angel.

The girl's angel handed out flowers to people who were on their way to heaven, to see Jesus "up close." A wonderful idea. The angel was preparing them for a spectacle. It's easy to understand why they smiled as they floated up with flowers. Imagine what they were going to see!

There's a word in the Bible for special times like this, a word for the kind of looking and seeing when we're face-to-face with God: "Behold!" The people in the girl's drawing were on their way to behold.

"Behold" is a special word. It means more than just "look" or "see." "Behold" is more like "I can't believe my eyes!"

When we read the word "behold" in the Bible, there is often an angel in the story. And when an angel says, "Behold," some amazing news is going to follow. Remember the angel's words to the shepherds? "Fear not, for *behold*, I bring you good tidings of great joy." And then the angel opened the shepherds' eyes to a baby born in a manger.

There must be lots of angels of behold, angels of marvel, of being astonished, of being overwhelmed. The job of an angel is to be God's messenger. And God's news is always marvelous, astonishing, overwhelming.

To behold God's messages is to feel a joy that goes beyond laughter or words. It comes when our eyes open to God's love, when we see so much and so far and so deep that we hold inside what we see. We want to keep those feelings inside. We are speechless with amazement.

Sometimes it takes an angel to help us behold.

The young girl drew an angel giving out flowers for heaven. An angel of behold. I wonder what that angel said to the people who were going to sit by Jesus. Maybe the flowers were enough: something to give Jesus when they behold him up close.

I wonder . . .

- ♡ if angels are ever speechless with joy.
- ♡ if silence can be a prayer.
- ♡ something can be so wonderful to make me speechless.
- ♡ when the angel of behold spoke to me yesterday.

What if . . .

- ♡ we would behold Jesus in church each Sunday?
- ♡ we could behold Jesus in our family?
- ♡ I reached out and gave an angel a hug?
- ♡ I remembered forever something good that happens today?
- ♡ we could help one another behold God's love and keep it inside?

Behold is . . .

- ♡ holding on to something you see so that it fills you up.
- ♡ being so glad you don't know what to say.
- ♡ when your words all come from your heart.
- ♡ when words get too big for your tongue.

Beholding together

Read three familiar stories in which God's angels of behold appear: Luke 1:5-24 and 26-38; Luke 2:8-18. Take turns reading the words of the angels of behold. Imagine how the listeners felt when they heard those eye-opening words.

Prayer

Be so glad over something today that you have nothing to say.

God, send me an angel to lead me to a surprise sight of you. Sometimes let me be so excited by your love that I have nothing to say to you. Help me be quiet when other people see something that makes them speechless. O God, slow me down to see more. Amen.

Angel of Earth

Angels know Africa,
Asia, and space,
Know all of the lands
of the whole human race;
The message of angels
is a message for all:
God's love came to earth
in a small manger stall.
The maker of heavens
and maker of all
Loves all of creation,
the great and the small.

Many children drew pictures of angels and the earth. The earth was usually a big ball that nearly filled the page. Land and vegetation were green, oceans and seas blue, and the sky and clouds were white. Some children drew angels sitting on the earth. Some had angels holding the earth up, like Atlas. A few drew angels reaching their arms around the earth, hugging it close.

Earth! What a creation. How do we grasp the meaning of the whole earth?

Do you remember first picturing the whole earth, looking at a world map or a globe, and trying to comprehend all the places at once? "Earth" means every single nation, nook, and cranny. Earth includes the great, wide sky, the hot fire deep down, and this place where we are right now.

Through the years I have written stories and songs about God's story. Sometimes I listed places where that story takes place: "Jerusalem, Bethlehem, Jericho, Omaha, San Francisco, Nazareth, Lake Superior, the Sea of Galilee." This combination of places startled some people. Think of it: God's story is happening in all these places—sometimes at at the same time!

Many people travel to the Holy Land to see where Jesus lived and preached and did miracles. And when they return, they discover that their home is also God's holy land: a place where God comes to calm seas, feed the hungry, heal the sick, proclaim good news. God's story has moved into their land, too.

When angels sang a song about "peace on earth," they sang about a peace that comes to all places, everywhere on earth.

Angels are pictured in the art and poetry of people all over the world. Angels come in all colors, kinds of wings, shades of halos, languages, and clothing. They are God's messengers everywhere, busy making sure God's story is told and heard in every country and nook and cranny on earth.

In Jerusalem, Bethlehem, Jericho, Omaha, San Francisco, Timbuktu, Tokyo, Anchorage, Paris, Melbourne, Moscow—and your living room, there are God's angels. Imagine!

I wonder . . .

- ♡ if angels ever need a map.
- ♡ how many languages angels know.
- ♡ if angels could be in more than one country at the same time.
- ♡ if I've ever met an angel from another country.

What if . . .

- ♡ the earth had a voice to speak?
- ♡ we were all part of one big country that covered the earth?
- ♡ Jesus had been born in our town?
- ♡ we could only rent the earth from God?

Earth is . . .

- ♡ where I live now.
- ♡ what grew when God started creating in the beginning.
- ♡ what God gave us all as a present.
- ♡ the one garden for all the world.

Places on earth

Let each person in your family or circle of friends choose a spot on earth—a country, city, island—and get to know it during the weeks ahead. If you've got a globe or world map, mark your spots. Read books and magazines about the place you've chosen. Listen to news reports about what's happening there. Pray for that spot on earth, for the people who live there, for the land itself.

Prayer

Find a a place in the news today, and know God is in that spot on earth.

O God, make every land and people a holy land on earth. Where we live needs healing and rest. Our friends need loving and care. Our family needs your healing and touch. I need to know that where I am you calm storms, you do miracles, and you listen. O God, make me well in your earth. Amen.

Angel of Balance

What is on the other end of an angel?" That is what I asked the children to draw during one of the days we met. One boy drew an angel standing at one end of a teeter-totter. At the other end was the earth. The teeter-totter was evenly balanced. The angel was smiling. The boy titled his drawing: "Heaven and earth come together, balancing on a teeter-totter."

These are his exact words: "Heaven and earth come together, balancing on a teeter-totter."

What is on the other end of an angel? The boy drew a teeter-totter, and an angel balancing the earth.

How is it that children are so profound in their journeys of the mind? How does God's Spirit form such imagination, such pictures of faith?

The teeter-totter was a great toy in my childhood. I liked it when another person and I were seated just right, balanced, so we could ride the long board fast and smooth. Up and down we'd go; or else we'd sway from side to side, suspended above earth. When that happened, I was right with the world. If I got on with somebody who was too light or too heavy, it was never as much fun. One of us would be grounded while the other was stranded in the air. We needed balance to have fun.

Many years later, I often rode teeter-totters with seminary students. These were word teeter-totters. One person would say a word at one end; the other had to say a word that would balance the first, a word that offset the other, an opposite word or feeling. Somebody said the word "sin"; somebody else balanced it by the word "grace." "War" was saved by the word "peace." "Broken" was saved by the word "forgiven." A teeter-totter of words.

Our lives are sometimes teeter-totters. We need God's angels of balance on one end to lift us up when we're feeling sad or bad or guilty. We need an angel to whisper about God's love and forgiveness and push us back up again. And when we get stuck up in the air, thinking we're better than others, not needing God, we need an angel of balance to tip us back down again.

God's angels of balance on a teeter-totter. Angels on one end, my world on the other. Isn't that a comforting thought?

I wonder . . .

♡ how long a teeter-totter can be.
♡ if there's a teeter-totter where feet never touch the ground.
♡ what's teeter-tottering inside me.
♡ what my two most different feelings are, and if they balance.

What if . . .

♡ a teeter-totter were as long as a life?
♡ grownups teeter-tottered more?
♡ enemies got on two ends of a teeter-totter?
♡ I teeter-tottered with an angel?

Balance is . . .

♡ when one thing depends on the other.
♡ when two opposites get along perfectly.
♡ how fun begins.
♡ when something is holding you up in the center.
♡ a feeling of peace.

Teeter-totter prayer

Take turns going down and up in a prayer of opposites. One person can begin by praying about something that is a "downer"—an angry word spoken, a feeling of guilt, a hurt suffered, an act of cruelty. Then it's your turn to add balance: speak words about God's forgiveness and love, talk about a kindness the other person has done, offer a genuine word of praise. Next, reverse roles and you pray about your own "downers." Be sure to end on an "upper."

Prayer

Think of strong words that lift you up when you are weak.

O God, thank you, for you have come to save everything, everything on earth and in heaven. You pick up what is broken and heal it. You keep something strong that needs not be weak. You turn something sad into a victory. You raised Jesus from the dead, and you balanced death with eternal life. O God, keep the teeter-totter in me balanced. Amen.

Angel of Circles

The child drew a circle of angels with wings touching. It looked like a Ferris wheel. Inside the circle of angels he drew another circle and colored the inside with faces of people: boys, girls, men, women, old people, young people, people of many colors. The angels formed a circle around all the people.

A circle of angels, a circle of people. I thought of the many circles of faces in all the world. I thought of families in their different kinds of circles.

We have all played circle games, laughing, enjoying life together. We hold hands around a table, pray together, and talk to God that way. We plant a tree, form a circle around the tree, sing a song, and begin to watch it grow. We baptize someone, give them a name, and stand around praying and taking pictures. There are times for making circles to sing, dance, cry, comfort, honor each other.

Family reunions look like circles. We stand around each other, feeling the ties that hold us together. Christmas looks like a circle, with animals and people around the child in a manger. I cannot imagine the birth of Jesus without angels, people, birds, and beasts around him.

At Easter, there's a tree or tomb in the center of the circle. At birth times, we stand around the baby, waiting for our turn to see or hold the child. When someone is hurt, we gather around the person to see how we might help. Sometimes we stand there just to be there.

Circles make us feel stronger. We add our strength to those on either side of us. They help us keep our balance. A circle can be a fortress, a protection. Castle and city walls were built in a circle. Strong walls surrounded, kept out danger, kept those inside safe.

Some churches are built like a circle. In this way, people see each other when they worship. They can take of each other.

I know a very smart teacher who draws God as a circle, and colors it like a rainbow. He sees God as being round, a wall of protection.

The child drew a circle of angels around a circle of people. Circles for caring and sharing. Circles for joy and fun. Circles for protection. A picture of God's love.

I wonder . . .

♡ how a circle begins or ends.
♡ why stems and branches grow round.
♡ when a family feels like a circle.
♡ if the church is a circle that circles.

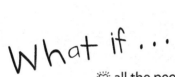

What if . . .

♡ all the people of the world stood in one circle?
♡ a house was built like a circle?
♡ a circle was a picture of God?
♡ a whole church were made of shapes of circles?

A circle is . . .

♡ when the beginning and end meet.
♡ how you can be hugged from every side at once.
♡ what can keep you safe all around.
♡ the shape in which most things grow.
♡ the shape of the mouth when it is surprised.
♡ how you sit so everyone can see each other.

Celebration of circles

Have a circle celebration. Serve circle foods such as donuts, bagels, pretzels, pizza. Sing favorite hymns in rounds: "All Praise to Thee My God This Night," "Beautiful Savior," "Praise God from Whom All Blessings Flow." Then have a circle prayer. Hold hands in a circle with one person in the center. Let each person in the circle pray for the one in the center. Take turns standing in the center until everyone has been surrounded and prayed for.

Prayer

Gather around something or someone and celebrate.

O God, circle us with your angels and bless us. Keep your angels around us on all sides. Help us feel loved today, tomorrow, and yesterday. Remind us to be a circle that cares around each other. Be above us, beneath us, behind us, before us, around us. Amen.

Angel of Time

One boy drew a picture of angels standing around a huge clock. The little and big hands of the clock were pointing straight up. It was midnight. The boy colored the sky dark blue around a moon and stars. Under the drawing he wrote: "It's time."

There is a song about time that has been around for years. It is in the Old Testament book of Ecclesiastes, and it begins "For everything there is a season, and a time for every matter under heaven." Time to be born, time to plant, time to build, to weep, to laugh, to dance, to seek. Minutes, hours, days, years, for living. We have time.

Time plays tag. One day touches the next day. Time unfolds, is filled, is fulfilled. There is so much time before us, around us, in us, ahead of us. The sky seems so new each day, and yet so old, so deep, so high, so far. To feel and to know this wonder of time is an honor. God honors us with the miracle of time.

Time is a magical toy. I fill my time in countless ways: living, working, playing, dancing, crying, worrying, loving, hugging, singing. I eat breakfast, practice piano, walk by a lake, lose my temper, say "I'm sorry," say "I love you." God gives us the toy of time, a gift of waiting, speaking, hoping, and living. Time stretches out in every direction.

In the New Testament, we read about time as also meaning readiness: "When the fullness of time had come, God sent his Son." The fullness of time, the right time. The thing time has been building up to.

The countdown to God's fullness of time began with Abraham. He looked for God's promised Messiah by counting stars in the night and grains of sands by the sea. People looked at the promise of God as though looking at a clock on a wall. Time was ticking off. They waited, they watched, for at the right time God would keep the promise.

The boy's angel clock pointed to midnight. He wrote, "It's time." Jesus was God's midnight, God's right time. We look back to Jesus as we look forward. Jesus is part of our minutes, hours, days.

And our time is full of God's love, older and brighter than stars, older and kinder than sands of the sea. God's love is deeper than the disappearing sky. To play with time, to live in God's time, leads us to give God honor.

I wonder ...

- ♡ if time can go in two directions at once.
- ♡ how time can seem fast or slow.
- ♡ how many kinds of time there are.
- ♡ where time goes when something has happened.

What if ...

- ♡ there were no clocks?
- ♡ I could tell time only by looking at nature?
- ♡ we were born with a timepiece inside us.
- ♡ time ran backwards?
- ♡ we could tell time by looking at each other's face?

Time is ...

- ♡ how we know how old we are.
- ♡ how God breaks up our life into wonderful pieces.
- ♡ how our life story has pages and chapters.
- ♡ how God keeps us surprised.
- ♡ what makes something very important.

Taking time

Take two full minutes to sit in silence and remember the ways you used the minutes and hours of your day. Tell God how you spent your time. Then take two more minutes of silence to plan tomorrow. Ask God to bless those plans and help you keep them.

Prayer

Keep your eye on a clock or watch, and pray.

O God, thank you for time—all kinds of time—in a day, in a week, in a month, in a lifetime. Thank you for creating time, and giving it to us in a way that we can divide it up, save it, look forward to it, and remember it. Thank you for right now, for yesterday, and for times to come. Fill up our time with good times. Amen.

Angel of Halos

Some angels go dancing
With candles as wings,
While halos make circles
Of bright yellow rings.

Halos are feelings,
Some halos are white,
Some look like bright music,
Some look like a light.

Most children used yellow when drawing angels. The yellow was for the angels' halos. Their halos were as tiny as a dot on a page, and large as a world. Sometimes they were stronger than the sun. Hardly ever was an angel without a halo, either as a lighted crown or around its body like a sunburst. Halo light came in all forms. One child turned the fire of a machine gun into angel light: an angel captured the fire and made it into a halo. One angel had candles for wings.

Halos are the light of God. This light belongs to us all and comes in many forms. Angels seem to wear a lot of it.

Halos are the way God shows in us. I felt this halo light through my mother. I heard it in the words of my father. I saw it in the faces of my neighbors.

Halos are God's energy and power, God's life, moving in the world. Halos are like sunlight, only brighter. Sometimes we see halos in the glow of a person's face or the sparkle in a person's eyes. Sometimes we hear halos in a tone of voice. Sometimes we feel halos in a group of people moving lovingly among each other. Sometimes we feel halos in a quiet person's presence.

Halos are a force and light above the power of candlelight and electricity and radiation. Halos are on the farthest, highest end of light. We call this very end of light Glory. Halos have higher vibrations than the highest pitch of a violin. Halos are the end of a sound we know as Alleluia.

Artists have pictured halos as rings and rings of glory around God's special beings—Jesus, angels, prophets, saints. Halos are rings of glowing light that come when a human spirit is on fire with God's Spirit. They are the fire and feeling of God's Holy Spirit. The rings of glory are like the fire of Pentecost that surrounded Jesus' disciples.

The sky was filled with halos one night over Bethlehem. That light is here tonight. And it can be seen in broad daylight. Each of us has a halo that grows brighter as we let God's light shine more and more.

Angels of halos. People of halos. God's glory light shines in us all.

I wonder . . .

- ♡ if halos are a kind of medicine.
- ♡ if halos come in all colors.
- ♡ if a hug can give me a halo.
- ♡ if halos can cover our whole body.
- ♡ if the light of halos goes inside.

What if . . .

- ♡ halos came in the colors of rainbows?
- ♡ you could give a halo as a gift?
- ♡ we could get a halo by loving someone?
- ♡ every baby got a halo at birth?

A halo is . . .

- ♡ a light that vibrates.
- ♡ God's energy that we can see.
- ♡ a decoration from God's Spirit.
- ♡ when someone's face glows with joy.
- ♡ my soul all around me.

Family halos

Give your family halos as reminders of the light of God you each carry. Cut out small circles of gold or yellow paper. Trim these to fit over the heads in a family photo or individual photos of family members. Tape the halos in place to the glass of the picture frame. How do the halos make you feel about one another?

Prayer

Feel or see or hear signs of glory today.

O God, shine brightly inside us. Pour your Spirit into us so we light up like Pentecost flames. Give halos to our voices and our eyes and our actions. Show us your glory, and let others see you in the halos we wear. Amen.

CPSIA information can be obtained at www.ICGtesting.com
Printed in the USA
BVOW06s1710210516

449027BV00009B/58/P